FOOTBALL

SKILLS & TACTICS

Wayne Rooney of Manchester United clashes with Pedro Mendes of Portsmouth during a Barclays Premiership match between Manchester United and Portsmouth at Old Trafford.

FOOTBALL

SKILLS & TACTICS

Written by: Edward Ensor
Consultant: Clive Gifford

Parragon
Bath · New York · Singapore · Hong Kong · Cologne · Delhi · Melbourne

This edition published by Parragon in 2010
Parragon
Queen Street House
4 Queen Street
Bath BA1 1HE, UK

ISBN 978-1-4075-9692-1

Printed in China

CONTENTS

Italy captain Fabio Cannovaro tries to block a shot by France's Thierry Henry during the 2006 World Cup Final.

INTRODUCTION

Millions of us live it and breathe it. When we're not watching our heroes, we're out there trying to play just like them. Whether it's a real match or a kickabout with some friends, we'd all love to score slick goals like Thierry Henry, defend as strongly as John Terry or dribble and pass like the Brazilian Ronaldinho.

If the top players have one thing in common, it's that they make difficult techniques look ridiculously easy. But we often forget that flashes of brilliance on the pitch are the result of hundreds of hours' work on the training ground.

Every player has to start with the basics, and that means practising all the key skills until they become effortless. This means your passing, shooting, defending and other key skills will hold up under pressure in a real match. This book guides you, step-by-step, through all you need to know about the game. There are plenty of tips to follow, tricks to try – and pitfalls to avoid.

Football is an action-packed team sport – the most popular in the world.

As well as looking at individual skills, you will also learn about tactics, and the importance of attacking and defending as a team.

Each section is fully illustrated. The photographs show some young players putting theory into practice, while some of the game's biggest names demonstrate how it's done – even in the heat of a competitive match.

So get reading this book and then get out there sharpening those skills. The more you practise, the better player you will become. You'll also increase your understanding and enjoyment of the world's greatest game.

WARM-UP

Portugal internationals Ricardo Carvalho and Simao Sabrosa demonstrate one way of stretching the hamstrings.

Footballers are an impatient lot. Whether it's just a kickabout in the park or a full-on competitive match, they are always desperate to begin play. But wait. Football is an extremely active sport. Often you'll be running non-stop, right from the start: other times you'll be standing around cold one minute then going flat out the next. Either way, you're less likely to play your best and are more likely to get injured if you don't warm up your muscles before play begins.

Watch the top players getting ready to come off the substitutes' bench and you'll see that they go through a vigorous warm-up session before joining the action. This is especially important in cold weather. Young players aren't quite so vulnerable to muscle strains and injuries, but it is still a good idea to start copying what the professionals do before they play – just as we all like to copy their tricks on the pitch.

Jog first

England squad members warm up during a training session at Arsenal's training ground.

The warm-up does two important things. It gets the heart pumping and the blood moving around your body. Then it prepares the muscles for the continuous cycle of contracting and lengthening they will go through during a football game. So the warm-up prepares the body for some explosive activity on the pitch and reduces the risk of injury.

You are more likely to get injured if you don't warm up your muscles before play begins.

A gentle jog is always a good place to start. You can build up the pace slowly, perhaps varying the length of your stride or raising your knees high, skipping or flicking your legs up behind you so that your heels touch your bottom. Some players also use star jumps, and swing their arms in a 'windmill' action to warm up and loosen their upper body. Work up to a sprint, by which time your heart rate will be up to the level needed for top performance.

High knee-lift

A high knee-lift run gets the heart pumping effectively and prepares the muscles for action.

Stretching out your quadriceps

Hold the stretch for 20 seconds. Repeat three times with each leg.

The quadriceps is the large muscle at the front of the thigh. Adopting the position shown (above), hold your ankle and pull it towards your bottom.

Make sure you are well balanced. If you need more support, try the position shown. You can also use a wall or goalpost to keep you steady.

Stretching

Football is a running game. A top player may run up to 12 kilometres in a single match. So, it is important to stretch all leg muscles including the calves, hamstrings and groin. However, loosening all the muscles is no bad thing. Stretching not only reduces the risk of injury, but also increases a limb's range of movement. Greater suppleness will be a distinct advantage during a game.

Get into good habits early on; make a thorough warm-up part of your pre-match routine. That way, you'll have less chance of getting caught cold when the whistle blows!

Get into good habits early on; make a thorough warm-up part of your pre-match routine.

The hamstring is the powerful muscle at the back of the thigh. It is quite easy to tear while sprinting.

Hamstring stretch

Stretch slowly down your body until you feel your hamstring tighten, then hold for 20 seconds.

Argentinean trio (left to right) Luis Gonzalez, Lionel Messi and Juan Roman Riquelme show the importance of stretching as part of the pre-match warm-up routine.

The calf muscle is at the back of the lower leg.

Calf stretch

Stand with one foot in front of the other. Keeping the back leg straight and the body as upright as possible, bend your front leg and move your weight forwards (left). Hold the position for 20 seconds.

TIPS

- Jog first - you should only ever stretch warm muscles.
- Stretch gently and slowly, and hold each position for 20 seconds.
- Never 'bounce' while stretching.
- Never overstretch. It will cause the very damage you are trying to avoid.
- Always 'warm down' after playing. Jogging and stretching are just as important at the end of a game.

After a game or training session, it is also important to reverse the process and 'warm down'. Five to ten minutes' jogging while varying your pace is ideal. Stretching all your muscle groups helps prevent them from stiffening up.

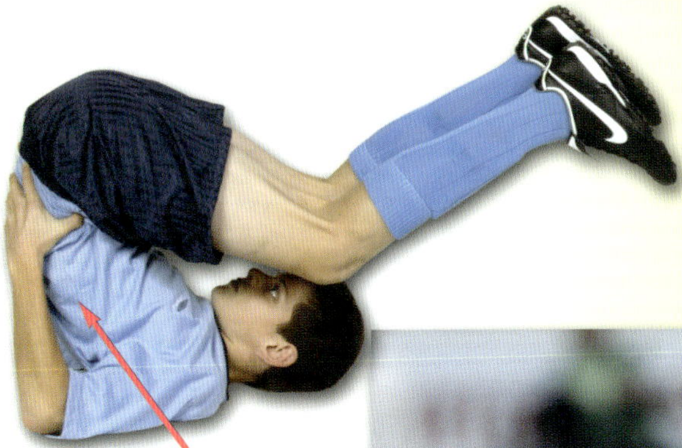

Back stretch

It isn't just the leg muscles that need warming up.

Groin stretch

Stand with legs wide apart, feet pointing ahead. Bend forward over one leg then the other, keeping them both straight.

Arouna Kone of the Ivory Coast stretches his groin muscles and hamstrings with an ankle grab.

STRIKING THE BALL

The techniques for passing and shooting are almost exactly the same. Both involve striking the ball. The only difference is where you want it to end up. With a pass, your target is a teammate; with a shot your target is the back of the net.

In a fast and furious game like football, the situation changes by the second.

The ball can be struck in a variety of ways, using a number of techniques. The technique you choose will depend on the situation, and in a fast and furious game like football, the situation changes by the second. A simple sidefoot pass might be on one moment but blocked by a defender the next. So you might decide to swerve the ball around your opponent instead. It is the same with shooting. You might plan to drive the ball past the goalkeeper, but if the keeper comes rushing out, you might decide on a chip instead.

Ronaldinho executes a perfect power drive. Note the position of the standing leg, head over the ball and use of the arms to aid balance.

Techniques for striking the ball

The ball can be struck with the inside or outside of the foot, the instep, the heel and even the toe occasionally. Every situation is different, and a player must use skill to decide which part of the boot he or she uses to deliver a particular pass or shot.

The most accurate way of striking the ball is with the side of the foot. Here, Chelsea's Michael Essien delivers a classic sidefoot pass.

The push pass

The basic sidefoot technique, where the ball is stroked along the ground, is known as the push pass. Despite its name, this technique works just as well in front of goal – by passing the ball into the net. The inside of the foot strikes the ball so that the foot is at right angles to the intended direction of the pass. The large surface area of the boot that touches the ball makes the push pass very accurate and reliable over short distances.

- The non-striking foot should be level with the ball.
- Weight should be over the ball on point of impact.
- The head should be steady, with eyes on the ball.
- The ball should be struck through its horizontal midline.
- The foot follows through in the direction of the pass.

The ball should be struck through its horizontal midline.

The push pass

The non-striking foot should be level with the ball as the inside of the striking foot meets it. The foot is at a right angle to the intended direction of the pass.

The drive

The lofted (upward) drive is more common in long passing, because the ball can sail over opponents' heads, making it difficult for them to reach. The low drive is ideal when shooting for goal.

For the low drive, place the non-kicking foot alongside the ball. Strike the ball with the toes pointing down. Hit through the centre of the ball, and follow through. Your body weight should be over the ball. This helps to keep the ball down.

When power and distance are called for, the ball should be driven with the instep.

For the lofted drive, the non-kicking foot should be slightly behind the ball. Again, toes should be pointing down on contact with the ball. Hit through the centre of the ball, but this time below the midpoint. Follow through. When driving the ball, either low or high, timing is much more important than brute force.

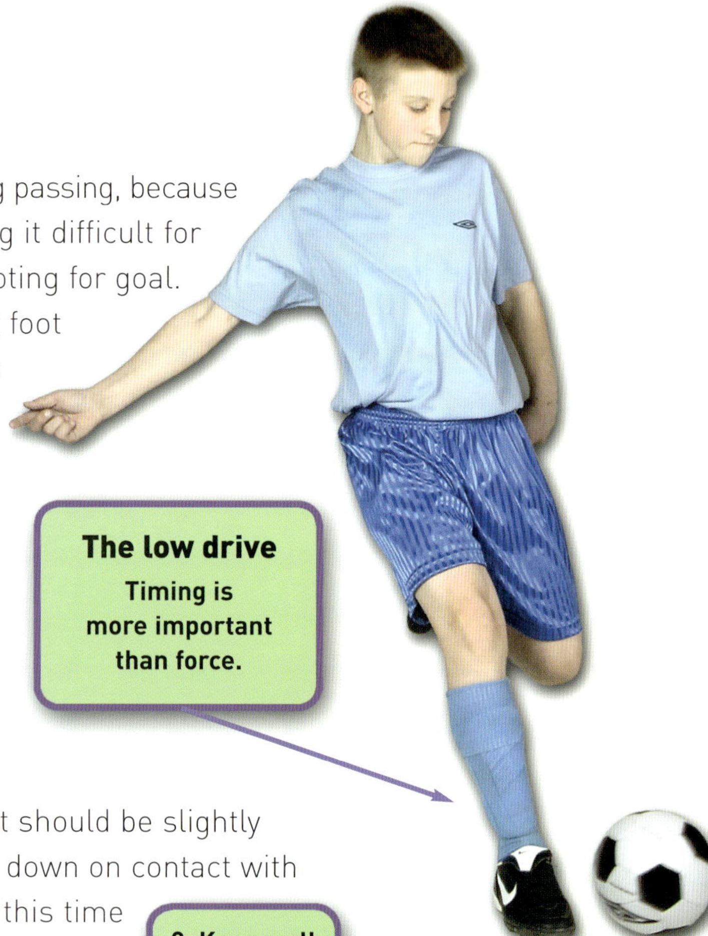

The drive

The non-kicking foot should be alongside the ball. Strike the ball with the toes pointing down, hit through the centre of the ball and follow through.

Swerving the ball

Striking the ball off-centre will give it sidespin and make it travel in an arc rather than in a straight line. The inside or outside of the foot can be used to swerve the ball in this way. For a right-footed player, striking the right-hand side of the ball with the inside of the foot will make it bend from right to left. If the same player strikes the left-hand side of the ball with the outside of the boot, it will bend from left to right.

Judging the amount of bend is one of the main difficulties of this technique. It will depend on the amount of pace and spin on the ball. Different types of ball and even atmospheric conditions can also have an effect.

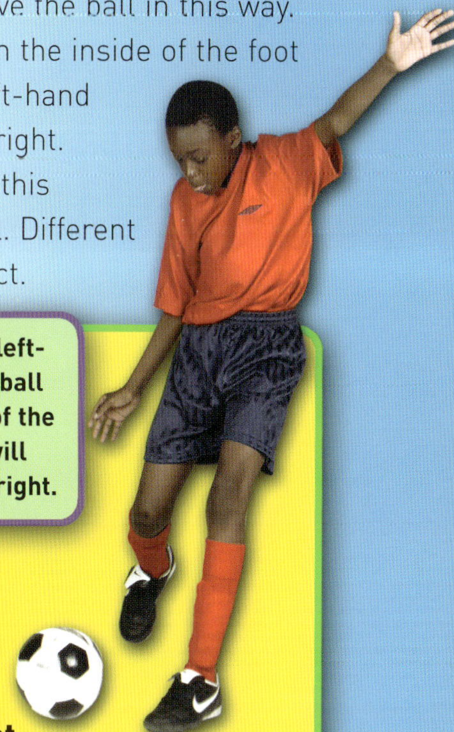

If you strike the left-hand side of the ball with the outside of the boot, the ball will bend from left to right.

Swerving the ball with the outside of the foot

Striking the left-hand side of the ball with the outside of the boot will bend it from left to right. Toes should be pointing down at point of contact. A long follow-through is very important.

Using the inside of the foot

- Practise bending the ball with the inside of the foot first, as it is easier to control.
- Strike across the right-hand side of the ball about halfway up (the left side if you are left-footed).
- As your foot makes contact it should rotate slightly, wrapping around the ball.

Using the outside of the foot

- To swerve the ball using the outside of the foot, toes should be pointing down at point of contact. The foot sweeps across the body from outside to inside, striking the ball about halfway up.
- The above technique will keep the ball low. If you strike the ball on either side but lower down, it will also swerve but will travel higher through the air.

Italy's free-kick specialist Andrea Pirlo swerves the ball by striking it off-centre.

The volley

If the ball comes to you in the air, you can either control it (see page 27) or strike it first time. The advantages of the latter – the volley – are speed and surprise. Whether you're trying to pass or shoot, striking the ball on the volley gives opponents less time to react.

There are three main types of volley. The first two are when the ball is in front of you or to the side. The third is when the ball is too high to reach and both feet are off the ground at the point of contact.

The power volley

Volleys can be hit hard to generate a lot of power and speed. For a front-on power volley, take your leg back, lift your knee and stretch your ankle with toes pointing down as the ball arrives. Keep your head forward and your body over the ball so it stays low. Leaning back a little will send the ball up higher, which can be of use when defending and clearing the ball from your penalty area.

The controlled volley

This sees the ball hit relatively gently with either the sidefoot or instep and used for a close shot or short pass to a teammate.

The power volley

Keep your arms outstretched for balance and your eyes on the ball. Make sure your head is over the ball to keep it low.

The side volley

Make sure you are well balanced on your standing leg. This is particularly important for a waist-high volley, when it is easy to fall away as you strike the ball. The body rotates around the standing leg as you make contact with the ball.

Strike the centre of the ball with the instep. Aim to make contact too high rather than too low, especially when shooting. If you get underneath the ball, it will balloon up in the air and over the bar. On the other hand, if you get over the ball, it will lose some of its pace but it still might be enough to beat the keeper.

TIPS

- The positioning of the non-striking foot is the key to a successful volley.
- Timing is more important than power.
- The follow-through is not as long as for a drive, but a smooth action rather than stabbing at the ball is crucial.

The side volley

Make sure your standing foot is in line with the ball. Give yourself enough space to strike the ball but remember not to overstretch.

Italy midfielder Daniele de Rossi strikes through the centre of the ball and remains perfectly balanced for this side volley, despite the attentions of France's Claude Makelele.

Overhead kick

The kicking foot should be at full stretch. Strike the ball using the instep, with the toes curled forward. Use the non-striking leg and the arms to break your fall as you hit the ground.

Timing has to be absolutely perfect. Even the slightest error can leave you flat on your back and the ball nowhere near its target.

TIPS

- Always practise an overhead kick on a soft surface.
- Overhead kicks must only be played when no opponent is close.
- Lean backwards before launching yourself into the air.
- The kicking foot should be at full stretch when contact with the ball is made.

Heel and toe

It is difficult to control the ball using the toe of the boot so it is best to avoid this technique whenever possible. The main exception is when going for a 50:50 ball. In these situations, stretching to toe-end the ball past an opponent might help you to keep hold of it.

Similarly, a striker going for a loose ball with an advancing goalkeeper might poke the ball past him to score.

Backheeling the ball is also risky but can be handy as it reverses the direction of play and takes opponents by surprise. Make sure you strike through the centre of the ball with your heel. An alternative is to roll the ball back using the sole of your boot.

The roll pass

Rolling the ball with the sole of the boot is accurate over short distances. It is often used to set up a shot from a free kick.

The chip

Players often find themselves needing to get the ball up and over an opponent but down quickly behind them. The chip shot sees the ball rise steeply but dip down sharply as it falls. On landing, the backspin on the ball stops it from racing away. The chip is useful for getting the ball over a keeper who is off his line, but down in time to enter the goal.

The non-kicking foot should be close to the ball, the knees slightly bent. The instep of the striking foot stabs down under the ball, and should make contact with the ball and the ground at the same time. There should be minimal follow-through. The chip is much easier with a stationary ball or one rolling towards you. It is more difficult if the ball is moving away from you.

The chip shot sees the ball rise steeply but dip down sharply as it falls.

The chip

The non-kicking foot should be close to the ball and the instep should make contact with the ball and the ground at the same time.

France's Zinedine Zidane scores with a clever chip from the penalty spot in the 2006 World Cup Final. Italy keeper Gianluigi Buffon dived early and Zidane chipped the ball into an open goal.

PASSING

Sandrine Soubeyrand of France makes a pass under pressure from England's Kelly Smith during a FIFA Women's World Cup Qualifier.

Everyone likes to see fantastic football skills in action: a snaking dribble, a flying header, a long range rocket into the top corner. But passing is the key to success. Four out of five times when you are an outfield player on the ball, your next move will be to pass to a teammate. Accurate, well-timed passing is essential to a team's success on the pitch. It links the players in a team and can turn defence into attack.

Successful teams like Manchester United and Arsenal have had many brilliant individuals. But both clubs' success is just as much down to their excellent passing play, which requires great teamwork.

Decisions, decisions...

When you have the ball, you should have a choice of players to pass to. You must decide which is the right option. Forward passes are essential to build an attack, but a sideways or backwards pass can be good if it keeps possession and changes the point of the attack. Playing with your head up makes you aware of what is going on around you, which helps you decide what pass to make. Each pass depends on the correct height, weight, direction and timing.

Sidefoot passes are very accurate. Make your pass as easy as possible for your teammate to receive.

The sidefoot pass

When you are an outfield player on the ball, four out of five times your next move will be to pass to a teammate. The sidefoot pass is the most accurate pass, and good over short to medium distances.

Height

Passes on the ground can often be delivered more accurately than passes in the air and are easier for the receiver to control. Passes in the air can be riskier and give defenders more time to react to make a successful interception. A well-hit aerial pass can cut out opposition players or help launch a quick attack by getting the ball to a forward in a space upfield.

Arsenal's Cesc Fabregas is well aware of teammate Robin van Persie's position. It is important that the player on the ball has a number of passing options available.

During a game there is often little time to make decisions because opponents react swiftly. Awareness of teammates' positions before you receive the ball is vital.

Weight

The weight of a pass is the amount of force with which it is hit and the speed with which it travels away. Not enough weight and the underhit pass may not reach its target. Too much weight and the ball may run out of play or be impossible for the receiver to control.

Direction

Many passes are aimed straight at the teammate, especially those in tight areas of the pitch full of players. But sometimes, a pass needs to be made to one side so that the receiver of the pass can cut away from their opponent to collect the ball. Other passes are aimed into space ahead of a speedy attacker, like Cristiano Ronaldo or Craig Bellamy, for them to run on to.

Timing

Even if a pass is carried out well, it may not be successful if it is made a moment too soon or too late. Timing is the shared responsibility of the passer and receiver. As receiver you must make yourself available and ready to accept the ball, and the player in possession must deliver the pass at that precise moment. Getting to know how your teammates play in training will help you to pass and receive in matches.

TIPS

- Practise estimating the weight of a pass. This is just as important as direction.
- Look to play the ball into a space for the receiving player to run on to.
- Keeping possession is essential – a pass backwards can be a positive move in certain situations.

Disguise

If you make it too obvious how you plan to play the ball, you might inform your opponents of that plan.

A range of tricks and techniques are used to hide a player's real intentions. Backheels can be used; players can look at one player and pass to another; dummies and feints can help to disguise where the pass is going. A disguised pass will give the receiver valuable extra time on the ball.

A range of tricks and techniques are used to hide a player's real intentions.

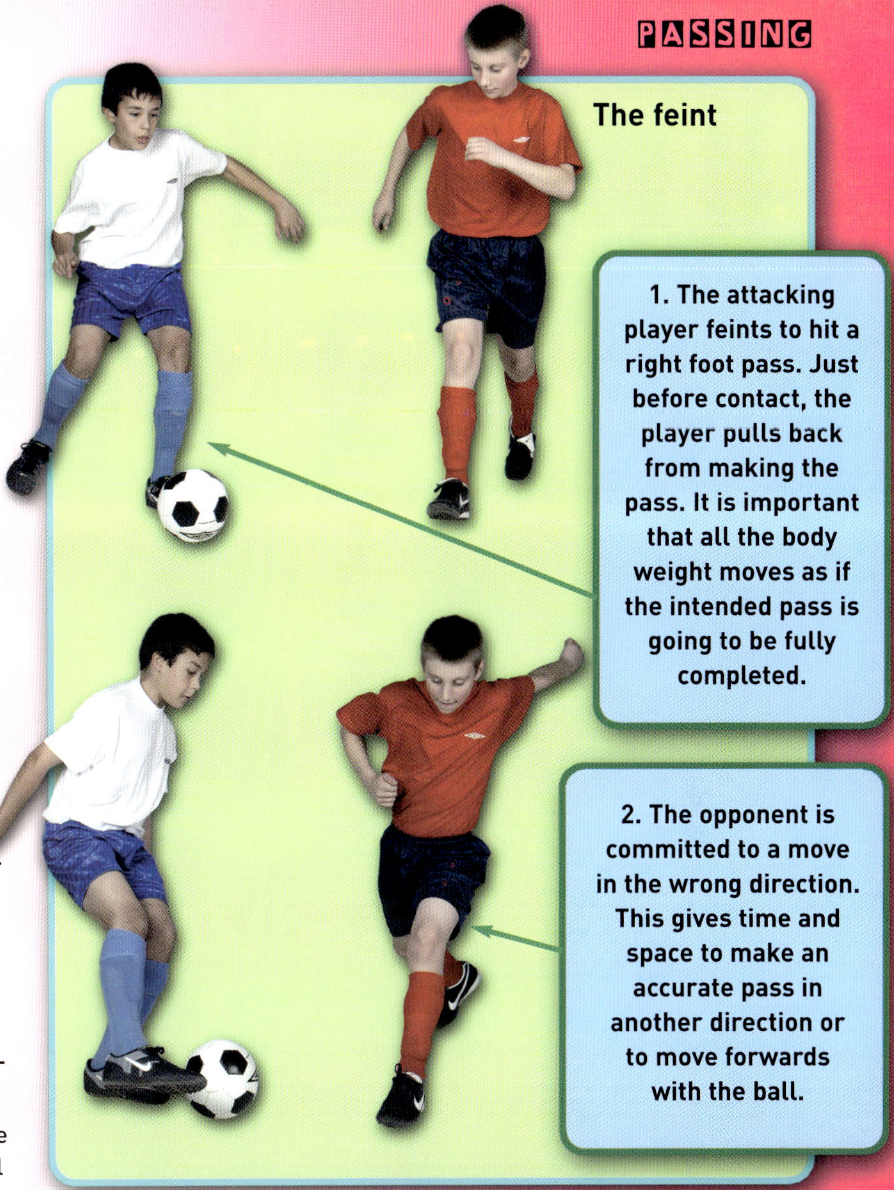

Chelsea players including Michael Ballack (left), Frank Lampard (centre) and Joe Cole (right) perform a quick, short-passing drill during training.

RECEIVING THE BALL

Passing and receiving are closely linked moves that glue a team's play together. One player's pass becomes a ball that has to be received by a teammate. A good pass puts the ball within easy reach of the receiver. But poor passes have to be received, too, so players need lots of practise in receiving balls that are spinning, bouncing awkwardly, travelling at great pace or coming at a difficult height.

Before the ball arrives, you should already have decided whether you are going to strike it first time or bring it under control. The less time you spend controlling the ball, the more you have to line up an accurate pass, shot or run forward. A player's first touch of the ball, whether it is with the thigh, foot or chest, is often crucial.

Italy striker Luca Toni takes a high ball on his chest during his side's victory over Australia at Germany 2006.

Good ball control buys you extra time and space to use the ball well.

Cushion control

The object with cushion control is to kill the ball's speed and keep it within your own playing distance.

If you allow the ball to cannon off you and rebound a couple of metres away, then the ball is loose and could be pounced on by the opposition. The part of your body making contact with the ball must be relaxed and must be moved away from the ball as it arrives to deaden its impact and leave it, usually, at your feet.

Cushioning a high ball to bring it under control.

Cushion control

It is important to get the body into the right, balanced position. The chest should cushion the ball so that the ball drops to the floor by your feet. Contact should be made with the large area of the chest, which is pulled back on impact to take the pace off the ball. Care should be taken to avoid contact with the arms.

Firm control

Often a player will want to take a high ball on the chest and push it into the space in front of him to run on to. Here, the chest is pushed out at the point of impact.

Keep the chest firm to steer the ball into space or pass to a teammate. Keep your arms and hands well away from the ball.

Firm control

Sometimes, players choose to keep some of the pace on the ball but change its direction.

Firm control can allow you to make an instant short pass to a teammate or propel the ball ahead of you to run on to. The surface touching the ball should be held relatively firm and thrust forward on impact, for example, when you want to keep the ball moving ahead of you.

Getting in line

Whether you choose cushion or firm control, the same rules apply. Decide which part of the body you're going to use to receive the ball as early as possible. Get your body in line with the ball. Go and meet the ball, don't wait for it to arrive. Use your body to shield the ball from your marker. Keep your eyes on the ball, but try to be aware of what is going on around you before the ball arrives. This is hard and only comes with experience and lots of practice.

Occasionally, even the best players get the balance all wrong between controlling the ball and thinking about what they are going to do with it next.

Don't stamp down on the ball hard or it may squirt out from under your foot. The position of the foot is the same as for a sidefoot pass.

Sole of the foot

Trapping the ball this way will bring it to a standstill. It requires perfect timing to ensure the ball doesn't bounce off the foot or slide underneath it.

Liverpool striker, Peter Crouch, shows good control to cushion the ball with his instep.

Top of the foot

This is only used when a ball is dropping from a height. The ball should be cushioned as the foot drops to the floor with the ball.

Instep

Only use this when it is impossible to get into the correct position with the side of the foot. With less surface area in contact with the ball, there is more chance of the ball bouncing too far away or going off at an angle.

Thigh control

Lower the leg to cushion the ball as it makes contact. This will bring the ball to rest at your feet instead of bouncing out of control.

Controlling the ball

To sum up, good control can be the difference between keeping and losing the ball, seizing the chance to attack or missing out. Top players are often praised for their ability to find time and space, even in the tightest games. These are usually players with excellent ball control.

Side of the foot

This is the most popular and effective way to control the ball. The broadest area of the foot meets the middle of the ball, bringing it to rest just in front of the player. The leg is moved back along the line of the ball's flight to take the pace off the ball and bring it to rest.

Ledley King of Tottenham Hotspur controls the ball during a Premiership game against Chelsea.

Newcastle United midfielder Scott Parker shields the ball from Fabio Rochemback of Middlesbrough.

Shielding the ball

Sometimes you will have the luxury of being able to receive the ball or play it while in plenty of space. More often you will have an opponent closing you down and looking for an opportunity to challenge. This is when screening or shielding the ball comes into its own. Quite simply, the golden rule is to keep your body between your opponent and the ball, thereby making it much more difficult for him or her to make a tackle without committing a foul.

If you receive the ball with an opponent close by, you should use your first touch to steer the ball away from them.

TIPS

- Once you sense a defender at your back try to keep them guessing as to which way you will turn.
- Shielding the ball can create valuable time for your teammates, to give you support and passing options.
- If your opponent is close to you, lean into them and roll your body against them to make a turn. (This is a particularly good option when you only need to gain a small amount of space for a shooting opportunity.)

1. To shield the ball, position your body between the ball and your opponent. Keep the ball under close control.

2. Be aware of where your opponent is and keep moving to ensure that your body stays between them and the ball.

3. You must not back into or push your opponent, but you can keep your arms out for balance. Look for your next move, whether it is a turn and sprint with the ball or a pass sideways or backwards.

Shielding the ball

If the ball is out of your playing distance, then blocking off an opponent in this way is obstruction and the referee will award a free kick to the opposition.

SHOOTING

Manchester United's Wayne Rooney lines up a shot. If defenders are prepared to back off, take the opportunity to shoot.

Football is all about scoring goals. Teams that don't make many attempts on goal are far more likely to struggle.

Liverpool's Steven Gerrard has a shot on goal past Middlesbrough's Fabio Rochemback during a Premiership match.

It is important to be aware of teammates in better positions than you, but don't pass on the ball and the responsibility when you get a good goal-scoring chance. If an opportunity to shoot arises, and it is within your range, then go for it.

The first thought of many great goal scorers is to have a strike at goal. Only if there is little chance of success are they likely to pass the ball on. Having made your shot, don't just stand there, follow the shot in. Many goals at all levels are scored on the second attempt, from a rebound or fumble from the goalkeeper.

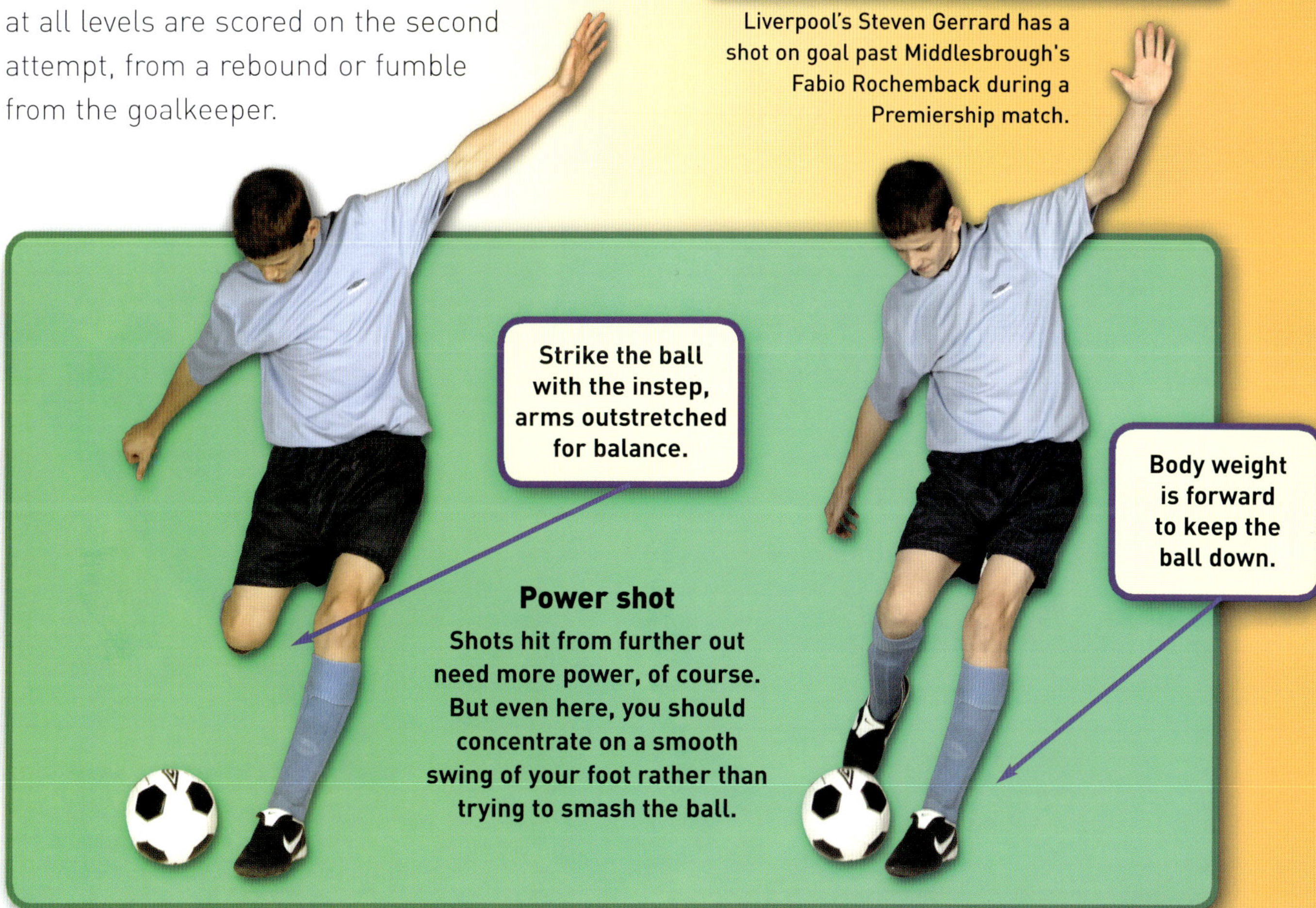

Power shot

Shots hit from further out need more power, of course. But even here, you should concentrate on a smooth swing of your foot rather than trying to smash the ball.

Shooting checklist

Go for it!

Never be afraid to shoot. The team that has most shots on goal wins more often.

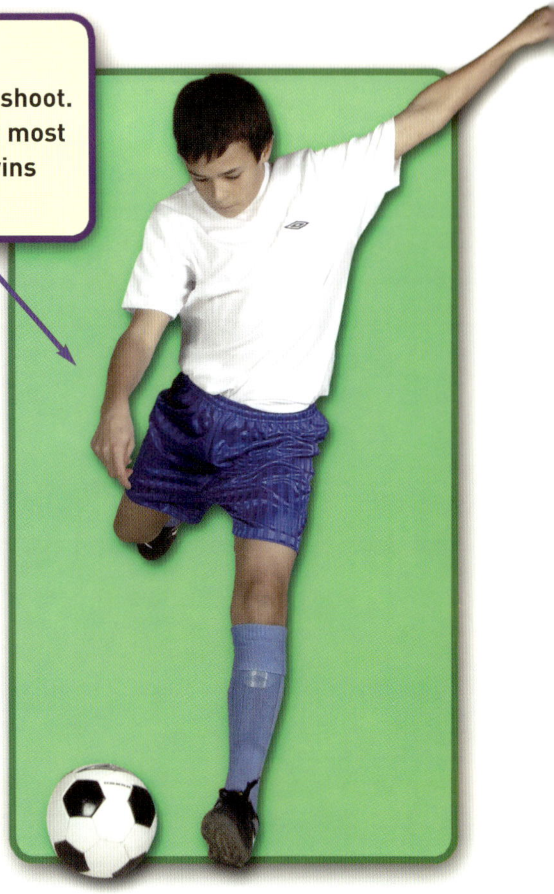

Be aware Keep your head up and your mind on the game. This will help you spot and react well to shooting chances.

Be confident Don't be afraid of failure. If you do miss, put it straight out of your mind and be just as confident the next time.

Be quick Chances come and go in an instant. Unconfident players are often guilty of hesitating on the ball or taking one touch too many; this can result in a good chance being lost.

Go low Aiming high for a thundering shot towards the top corner of the goal may look spectacular, but such a shot is often saved as it arrives at a good height for a goalkeeper – or it may miss altogether. A low shot into the corner or into an empty part of the goal is often more effective, and may also lead to a deflection.

Placement versus power
For close-range shooting, accuracy comes first, power second. Shots hit from further out need more power, but even here, you should concentrate on a smooth swing of your foot rather than trying to smash the ball.

TIPS

- Don't be afraid of failure.
- Regularly practise shooting with your weaker foot.
- Never waste a chance to shoot first time.
- The goal never moves, so be aware of where the target is at all times.
- Keep composed even under the pressure of a vital scoring opportunity.

For close-range shooting, placement is more important than power. Here, Lionel Messi sidefoots the ball into the net during Argentina's 6-0 win over Serbia and Montenegro at Germany 2006.

Use both feet

If defenders know you will only go for goal with your stronger foot, they will cover that side and make shooting difficult. Work hard on shooting well with both feet so that you offer double the threat and can shoot from both sides.

Anticipate Good strikers seem to know instinctively where the ball will fall, and position themselves accordingly. Even if you haven't reached that level yet, try to guess the outcome: will a teammate win a header or will the ball bounce off the goalposts or the goalkeeper and reach you?

Tottenham's Jemain Defoe fires off a shot before he is tackled by Hayden Mullins of West Ham during a Premiership match.

Placement and power

Chances come and go in an instant. Be ready – half of all goals scored are from first-time shots.

DRIBBLING

Arsenal's Theo Walcott uses his pace and trickery to wrong-foot the Swiss defence in an England Under-21 international.

Dribbling is all about using close control skills with the ball to take on and beat one or more opponents. Players usually have their own special ways of beating an opponent, but there are also some moves and techniques that are often used by most players.

Dribbling is a risky business. Even the very best, like Cristiano Ronaldo, run out of luck eventually. It is better to dribble past one player and then release a good pass than to beat three players only to lose the ball to the fourth. Because of these risks, dribbling is best performed only in the attacking third of the pitch. It can be very useful when all your teammates are marked. Dribbling may force more than one defender to come and challenge you for the ball. This may leave a teammate in a space to receive a pass.

Turning

Turning with the ball is a skill that is often underestimated and not practised enough. This is a mistake as the ability to turn quickly can help a player beat an opponent or get an attacker to face goal ready to shoot. You can change your direction by running around the ball, standing on one foot and pivoting around with the other or by using a hook turn.

Germany's Lukas Podolski beats his opponent with a hook turn using the inside of his foot.

Hook turn

When marked from behind, you can turn round the defender, hooking the ball with the inside or outside of your foot so that the ball travels with you.

1. To perform a hook turn with the outside of your foot takes good balance.

2. As you receive the ball, plant one foot. Reach across your body and control the ball with the outside of your other foot.

3. Drop your shoulder and lean in the direction you want to turn. Hook the ball at its bottom and sweep it round. Turn quickly to follow the ball and move away sharply with the ball under control.

Successful dribbling

It is important to keep the ball under close control because kicking the ball too far ahead will make the defender's job easy. Hold up your head so that you can keep an eye on the whereabouts of your teammates and opponents at all times.

The three key points to successful dribbling are to keep close control of the ball, keep your head up and play the ball with both feet.

Most players have a stronger leg, but if you always use that one to play the ball, the defender will know what to expect from you. Similarly, don't try to beat a defender on the same side every time. The more you can keep your opponent guessing, the better your chances will be of getting past him or her.

Dropping the shoulder

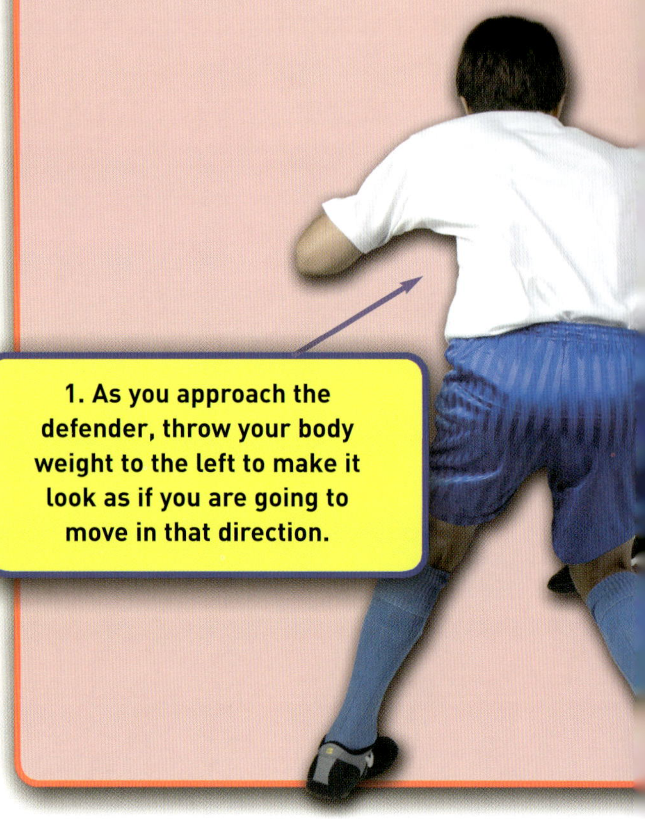

Attack with pace An opponent running at pace with the ball under control is a defender's nightmare. If you're not very fast, try to vary your pace to keep the defender guessing.

Change direction Twist and turn to keep a defender on his or her toes. The more often they have to change their stride, the more chance you have of putting them off balance.

Shield the ball Whenever possible, keep your body between the defender and the ball. This will make it harder for them to take the ball without committing a foul.

Use feints and dummies Pretend to make one move but really do another. Any movement that sends your opponent in one direction while you speed off in another is very useful.

The step-over

2. An exaggerated drop of your left shoulder fools the defender into thinking you plan to go that way.
3. As the defender reacts, swerve in the opposite direction and accelerate past him on the right.

2. Instead, swing your foot over the ball and plant it on the ground.
3. Push off this foot and go past your opponent on the left, playing the ball with your left foot as you do so.

Feinting

Feinting involves fooling your opponent into thinking you are going to go one way, then moving off in a completely different direction. You can do this in a lot of ways, but the common element in all cases is the use of exaggerated body movements. Defenders are supposed to concentrate on the ball, not on the movement of the body, but even the best defenders will react to body movements. Trying to fool a defender in this way is also known as 'selling a dummy'. Make your movement convincing. Remember, the point is not to show off but to beat a defender and to set up an attack. Watch top players such as Ryan Giggs and Ronaldinho, but work on moves that best suit you and your skills.

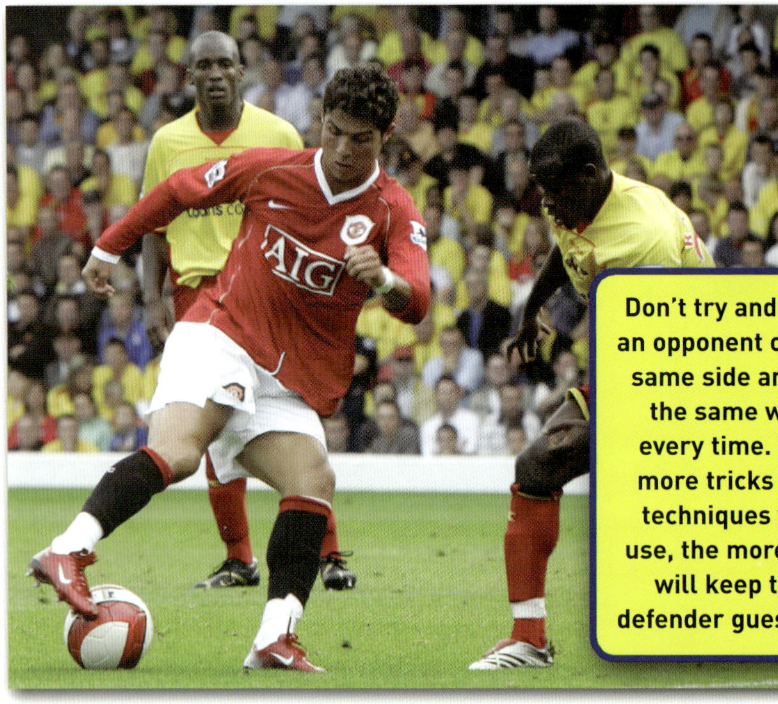

Don't try and beat an opponent on the same side and in the same way every time. The more tricks and techniques you use, the more you will keep the defender guessing.

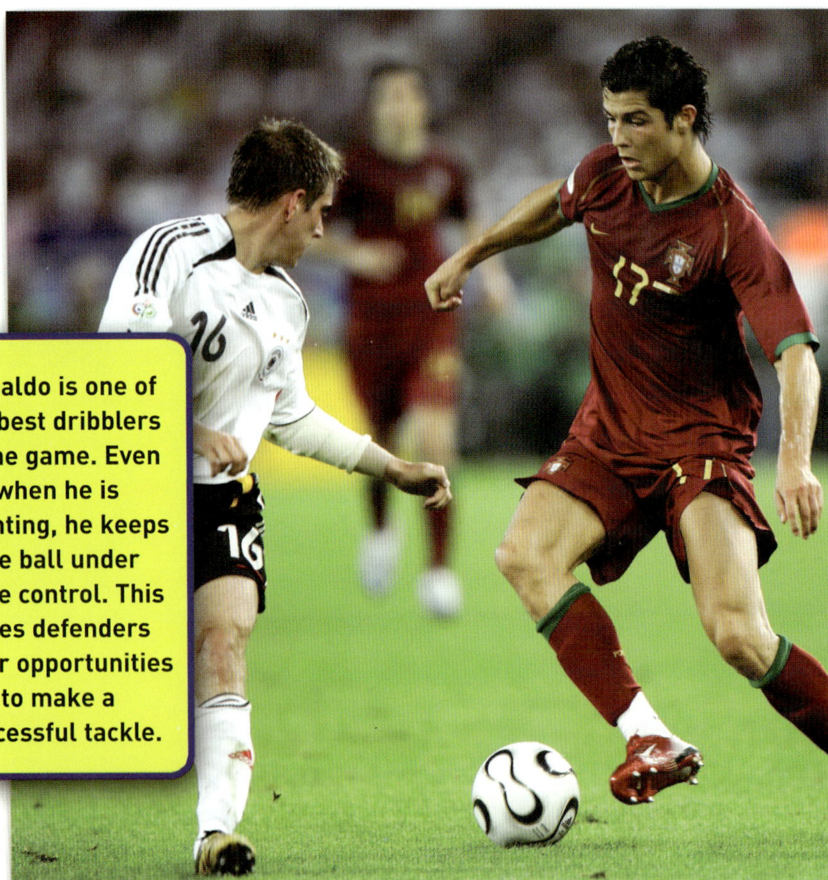

Ronaldo is one of the best dribblers in the game. Even when he is sprinting, he keeps the ball under close control. This gives defenders fewer opportunities to make a successful tackle.

Above: Cristiano Ronaldo of Manchester United tries to beat Alhassan Bangura of Watford.

Left: Ronaldo dribbles the ball for Portugal against Germany in the 2006 World Cup.

TIPS

Dribbling practice:

- Remember to use the inside and outside of both feet.
- Don't kick the ball too far ahead of you.
- A lot of light taps of the ball are better than a few heavy ones.
- In training, don't concentrate on the ball so much that you don't know the position of the next cone. (Or, if it were a game, the next defender).
- Play with your head up.

The dragback

This is when the attacker uses the sole of the boot to draw the ball back and reverse the direction of play. It is especially effective if you are running alongside an opponent at pace. As you suddenly stop and drag the ball back, your opponent sails past you and, for the moment at least, is no longer a threat.

Practising

Dribbling skills need large amounts of practice. One good way is to weave in and out of a line of cones. Space them fairly wide apart at first, as these will be easier to get around. As you improve, you can bring them closer together. This will make the turns a lot tighter and really test your close control.

Feinting is an important part of the dribbler's art.

Spain's Fernando Torres skips between two Liechtenstein defenders in a Euro 2008 qualifier. Dribbling isn't just exciting to watch, it can take defenders out of the game and create a goal-scoring opportunity.

TACKLING AND DEFENDING

Tackling covers the techniques you can use to try to win the ball from an opponent. Defending is a much wider subject. It involves decision-making and taking up positions that will help your team win the ball or prevent your opponents from using it to their advantage.

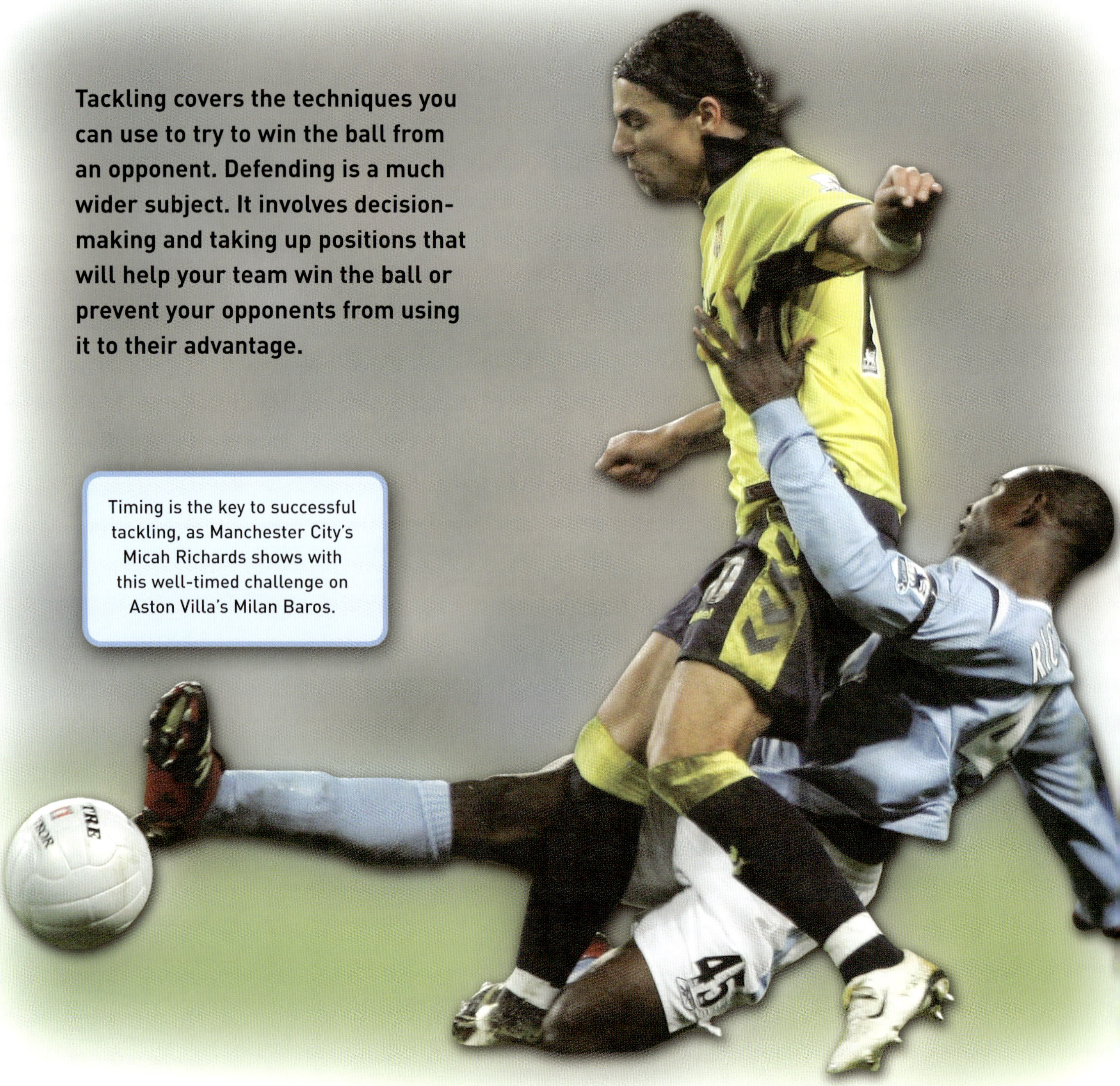

Timing is the key to successful tackling, as Manchester City's Micah Richards shows with this well-timed challenge on Aston Villa's Milan Baros.

Tackling

Watch the ball, not any feints or dummies that your opponents might throw. Keep moving yourself into the best position while you are waiting for the right moment to strike. This includes using your body position to manoeuvre your opponents into less dangerous areas.

You should challenge for the ball when you feel confident of winning it.

When you decide to make a tackle, the important factors are speed, determination, accuracy and timing. If either of the first two factors are lacking, then you have less chance of winning possession. If your tackle is clumsy, off-target or you get your timing wrong, you risk fouling your opponent and giving away a free kick, or a penalty if inside your penalty area.

Good defenders are always ready to intercept the ball.

Interceptions

Be alert for an underhit or misdirected pass. If you can steal the ball before it reaches the intended receiver, you won't need to tackle him.

Avoid fouling

Try and win the ball cleanly. If you make contact with the player first, it's a foul.

Miroslav Klose of Germany challenges Andy Selva of San Marino for the ball during a Euro 2008 qualifier.

The block tackle

The block tackle is the most common challenge in football. It can be made from the front or the side, but in both cases the side of the foot is used to block the ball.

If both players meet the ball at the same time, it isn't necessarily the biggest or strongest player who will come away with it.

In a front-on tackle you should put your standing foot beside the ball and lean into the challenge with your full body weight driving through the tackling leg. Block tackling from the side needs good timing, or your opponent will skip clear. To perform a side block, bend your supporting leg and use your other foot to hook the ball away from your opponent's feet. Your shoulder may make contact with your opponent. This is okay as long as you make contact with the ball. But don't barge or force the player over or the referee will blow for a foul.

The block tackle

When you arrive at the ball at the same time as your opponent, first ensure a good body position with your weight over the ball.

1. To win the ball, you must get as much of your foot in contact with it as possible. Your full body weight should drive through the tackling leg.

2. If the ball gets stuck, push the ball and roll it up and over the top of your opponent's foot.

The roll-over

The slide tackle

When tackling, try to stay on your feet. Once you go to ground, you are out of the game. Only commit to a slide tackle if you are certain of winning the challenge. The reason for this is that most slide tackles are made from behind and are risky. You must make sure that you do not contact the attacker's leg before connecting with the ball, or the referee may give a free kick or penalty. Most players try to use the leg furthest away from the attacker to make the tackle as this gives you more balance and a stronger tackling position. If the timing is perfect, you can hook your foot around the ball and cradle it there throughout the tackle to keep possession. The aim with many slide tackles, though, is to remove the ball from the opponent's control and out of play.

If your team loses the ball, every player becomes a defender. The strikers are the first line of defence, as Arjen Robben shows with this challenge on Emmanuel Eboue.

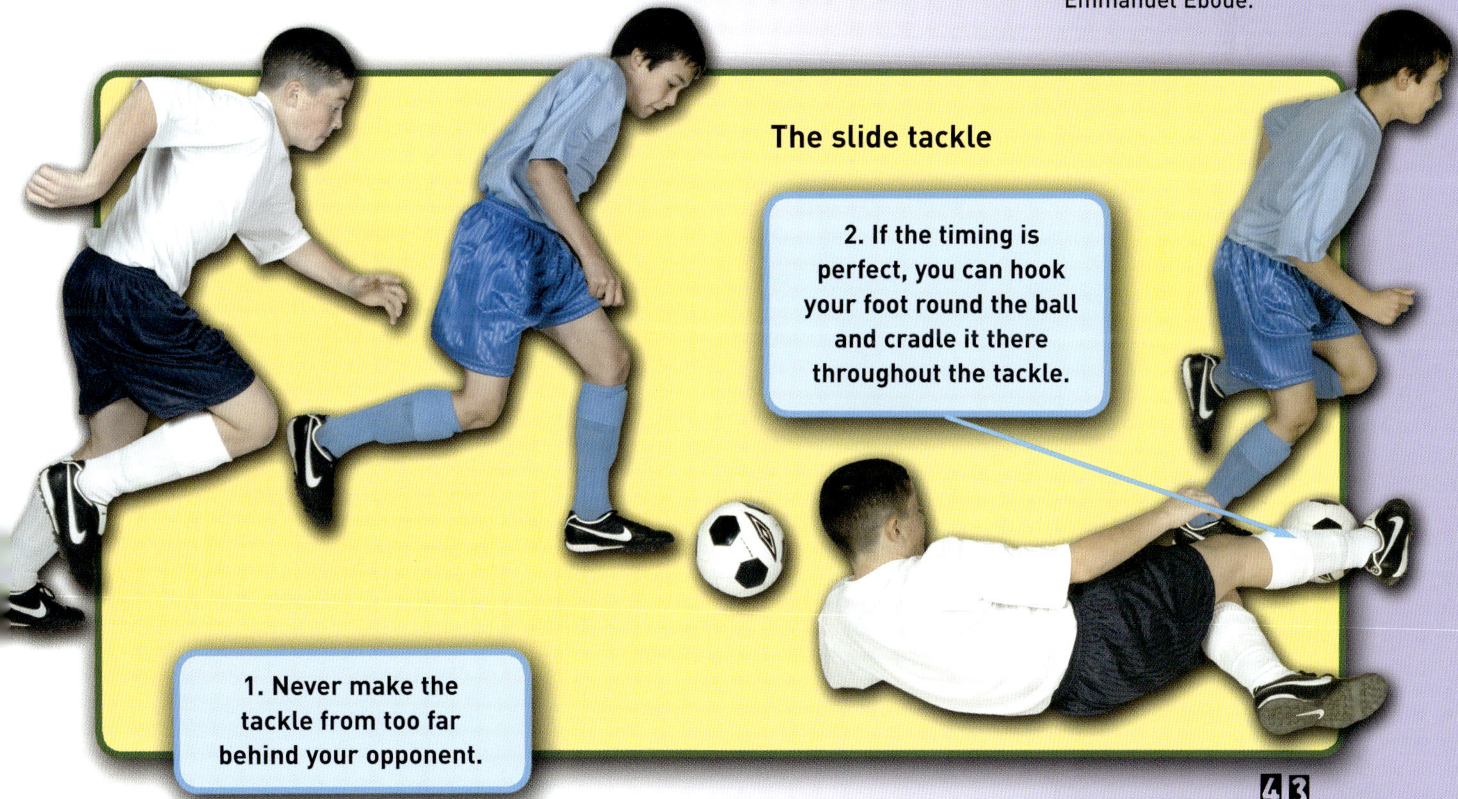

Defending

Defending is not just for defenders. When the opposition are in possession, good teams defend from the front. This means that strikers should be the first players to pressure their opponents with the ball.

Defenders often mark an opponent closely to deny him or her the space to receive the pass. As a defender you must strive to stay between the opponent and your own goal to make it harder for the opponent to shoot. An attacker often receives the ball with their back to the goal they are attacking. As a good defender, you need to react quickly to try to prevent the attacker from turning. You should aim to get about one metre from your opponent and stay goalside. You should try to keep the ball in view as you prevent the turn.

The strikers may not get a tackle in, but they can deny their opponents time and space and maybe panic them into making a mistake.

Prevent your opponent from turning

A player receiving the ball will be a greater attacking threat if allowed to turn. As a defender, you should react quickly and aim to get within one metre of your opponent by the time the ball arrives. If you hang back any further, the attacker will have room to manoeuvre into a good position to pass, dribble or shoot. If you get too close, it will be difficult to keep the ball in view, and a quick move from the attacker could take him or her out of range before you have time to react.

Arsenal's Thierry Henry finds himself up against two Barcelona defenders in the 2006 Champions League final. 'Doubling up' on a dangerous player does carry risks, though, as it may leave another attacker unmarked.

1. Standing on the balls of his feet, the defender jockeys his opponent. His body weight is over his knees, which are flexed. He is ready to move in any direction and keeps a distance between himself and his opponent. He watches the ball closely.

2. As the attacker moves, so does the defender, trying to delay him and force him to the sideline. The defender stays between the attacker and the goal all the time. Any mistake from the attacker and the defender might swoop to gain the ball.

Force your opponent into a less dangerous area

A defender tries to jockey and delay their opponent and drive them across field or to the sidelines and away from good attacking positions. In doing so, the defender may also buy their teammates extra time to get back into good defensive positions.

Jockey and be patient

Even if the attacker has been able to turn, it is still up to him or her to do something with the ball. The longer they keep the ball, the more chance of making a mistake. Don't dive in unnecessarily and solve the problem for them. Be patient and wait for a momentary loss of control, when the odds will be stacked in your favour to win the ball.

Real Madrid defender Sergio Ramos steers an attacker down the line while waiting for the right moment to make a tackle.

HEADING

Tottenham Hotspur's Didier Zokora climbs high to head the ball in a Premiership match against Chelsea.

Football purists often say that the game is supposed to be played on the ground, not up in the air. They don't like to see a lot of aerial 'ping-pong'. But sometimes a high ball is exactly the right option to choose. Once the ball is in the air, both teams will want to challenge for it. If you wait for the ball to drop, you run the risk of losing possession, or maybe even allowing the other team to score a goal. No matter what the purists say, heading is a skill that can win and lose games.

Much of a game of football is played on the ground. Once the ball is in the air, both teams will want to challenge for it. Heading is a crucial skill that can gain possession, launch or stop attacks, score goals and win games. Heading a ball doesn't come naturally to some young players, but can be learnt and practised. There are four main pointers to follow to make a good header.

- **Use your forehead** By making contact with the ball above the eyes you will be able to watch the ball right up to the moment of impact. It will make controlling the direction of the header easier and, done well, won't hurt.
- **Keep your eyes open** Photographs show that even professionals close their eyes at the precise moment of contact between head and ball. This is normal, but you should try to keep your eyes on the ball for as long as possible. Watch the ball on to your head.
- **Arch your back, nod your head** In many cases, you will be trying to get maximum power into your header. By arching your back and snapping forward at the point of contact, you will give your head forward momentum when it meets the ball. Even more power is generated if you also use your neck muscles to punch through the ball at the same time.
- **Attack the ball** Be positive, be first to the ball. Meet the ball and don't let it hit you. If you wait, the chance of an opponent getting to it first increases.

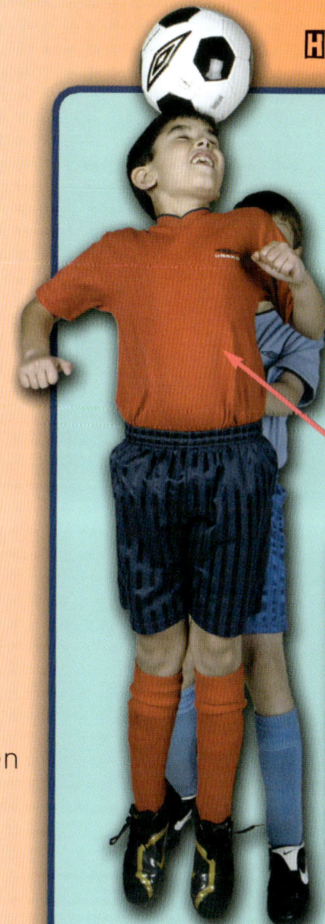

Flick-on
You can use the top of your forehead and head to flick the ball on to a teammate behind you.

Statistically, about 20 per cent of goals are scored from headers. That figure was 66 per cent in the 1998 World Cup Final. Two of the three goals that brought France victory came from the head of Zinedine Zidane.

You don't have to be tall to be good in the air; timing, technique and having good 'spring' are the most important factors.

Arsenal's Robin van Persie twists in the air and uses his neck muscles to power his header towards the goal. Notice that the ball is travelling downwards, which will make the header more difficult for the keeper to save.

Different types of header

Defensive header

This header is used for clearing the ball away from your goal and out of danger. You are aiming for maximum power to head the ball up but mainly forwards to get it as far away as possible. Try to make contact just below the middle of the ball. If you contact the ball well above its middle, you're more likely to head it down into the path of an opponent. If you head the very bottom of the ball, you may send it straight up and still be in danger.

TIPS

Practising headers:

- Putting all four of the key points into practice with a moving ball is very difficult. Work on good technique with a static ball first.
- Always hold the ball at a suitable height.
- When you are timing your headers well in this way, you can move on to heading balls thrown gently by a partner.

Heading for goal

Accuracy is vital with an attacking header. Getting above the ball to head it down is crucial. Not only does that help prevent the ball from sailing over the crossbar, it can also be harder for a keeper to save. Aim to connect with the ball just above its middle.

If you are meeting a cross (a high pass from a wide position) you have a number of choices. You can try to meet the ball strongly and aim inside the goal at the near post. You can use the top of your forehead and head to flick the ball on to a teammate behind you. You can also attempt a glancing header to deflect the ball across goal and into the net near the far post. Glancing headers are tricky to get right but can be devastating in front of goal. Statistically, about 20 per cent of goals are scored from attacking headers.

Challenge for the ball when it is in the air rather than risk losing possession.

Cushioned header

This is used when passing back to your goalkeeper or when you want to set up a teammate nearby. The key thing is to relax your neck and shoulder muscles and to bring your head back as you connect with the ball. Your aim should be to remove most of the ball's speed as it travels gently to your teammate.

Barcelona defender Carlos Puyol (left) outjumps AC Milan's Filippo Inzaghi to clear the ball from the danger area. With a defensive header it's important to go for power and distance.

Defensive header

Keep your eyes open and watch the ball right up to the moment of impact. Use your arms as levers to help your jump, but be careful not to raise them too high or hit another player. For a defensive header you should try to make contact below the horizontal midline of the ball. Too high and you'll head the ball down, possibly to an attacker. Too low and the ball will go up into the air but won't travel far.

TIPS

- Meet the ball, don't let it hit you. If you head the ball properly it won't hurt you.
- Keep your eyes on the ball at all times.
- Where possible, head from a standing position for better balance.
- As the head goes forward the arms go back and down for leverage. Take care with your elbows to avoid fouling.

Attacking header

A downward header poses most problems for a goalkeeper. Contact with the ball for an attacking downward header should be just above the horizontal midline. Go to meet the ball; don't let it hit you.

Sevilla forward Julien Escude dives for a header in front of Barcelona goalkeeper Victor Valdes during the European Super Cup.

If you really launch yourself at the ball, a diving header can be as powerful, effective and spectacular as a kick.

GOALKEEPING

As the last line of defence, goalkeepers can grab the glory, but are also under a lot of pressure. Brilliant saves can win games, but mistakes are often punished and can lose games as well.

Czech Republic keeper Petr Cech dives bravely at the feet of Ghana striker Asamoah Gyan and safely gathers the ball.

Agility to make dives and leaps, fast reactions and excellent handling skills are all things a good goalkeeper needs. Goalkeepers must also be brave and prepared to dive low for a ball in an area where other players' boots might be flying.

Keepers need strong powers of concentration. They may be asked to do nothing for a long period then suddenly pull off a spectacular save or face a high-pressure one-on-one situation.

Goalkeepers can often help protect their goal without making a save. They do this through communicating with their defenders and directing them clearly. Staying alert and aware, the keeper often has the best view of an opposition attack.

A keeper who makes quick, clear decisions and communicates orders well to his defenders is said to be in command of his penalty area.

Ready position

A goalkeeper's ready position sees you well balanced on the balls of your feet and ready to move quickly in any direction. Hands should be held out at about waist height and eyes should be on the game ahead.

Keep focused. Goalkeepers may have little to do for long periods, so concentration is especially important.

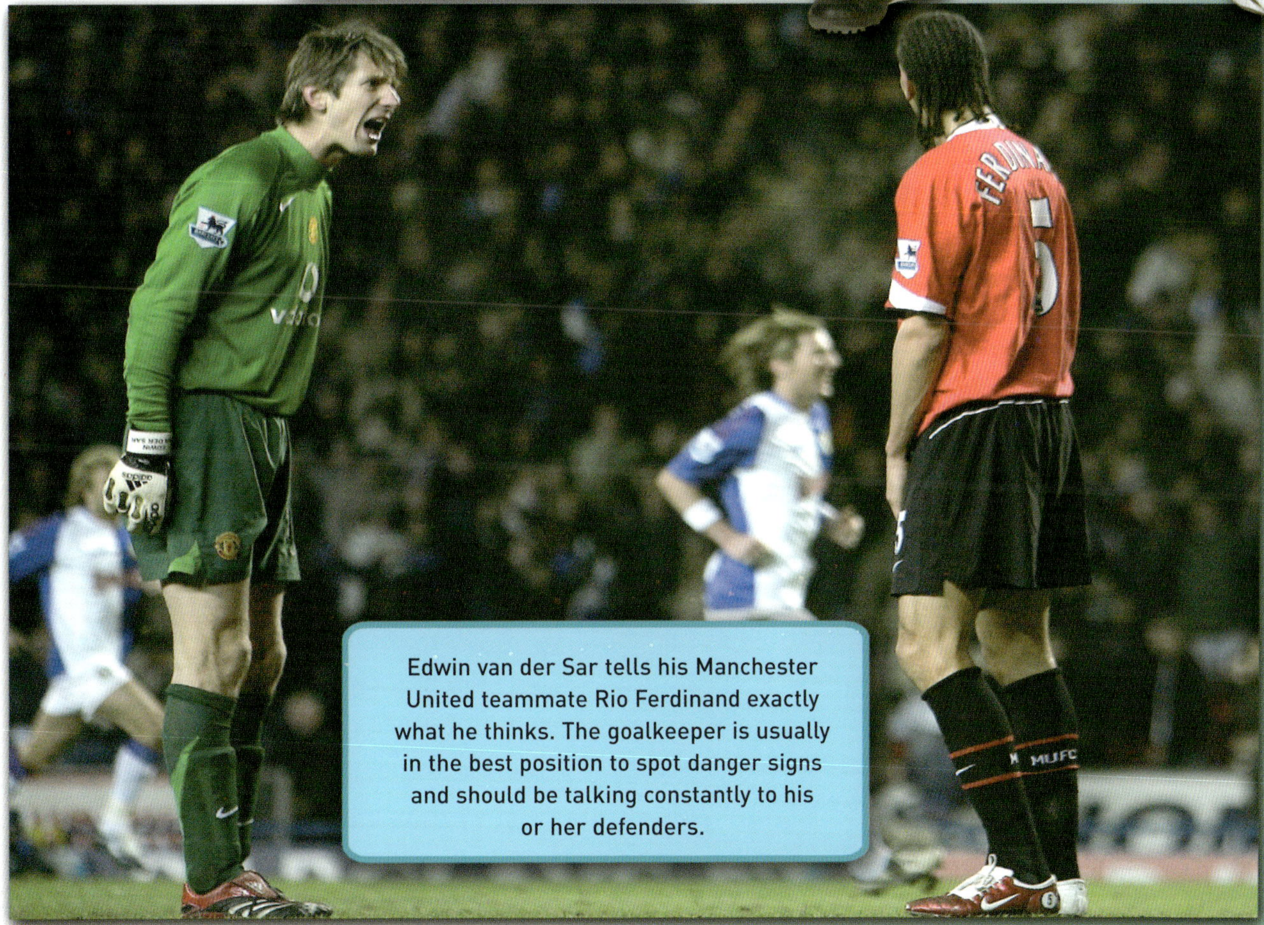

Edwin van der Sar tells his Manchester United teammate Rio Ferdinand exactly what he thinks. The goalkeeper is usually in the best position to spot danger signs and should be talking constantly to his or her defenders.

Shot stopping

As a goalkeeper, you should get as much of your body as possible behind the ball. Two hands are therefore better than one, and if the body is behind the hands to provide a second barrier, all the better. Of course, this isn't always possible and getting anything behind the ball is important. This might be a hand, the fingertips, or even an outstretched leg.

Diving

If the ball is high and to your right or left, try to push off with the leg that is nearest to the ball and aim to get both hands on it if possible.

Shots along the ground

For shots along the ground most keepers tend to drop one knee and scoop up the ball with both hands. Others bend their back and stoop to take the ball.

Low shots

For shots between knee and waist height, get the body behind the ball and use the scooping technique to bring it into the chest. If the shot is low, the body will naturally topple forward, but the ball will be safely cupped to the chest before you hit the ground.

One hand

If you can only reach the ball with one hand, make contact with the open palm and outstretched fingers. Guide the ball over the bar or round the post.

Collecting a ground ball

To collect a low ball, keepers drop down on to one knee and lean forwards a little. Getting your body in line with the ball's direction to act as a barrier, gather the ball in with outstretched hands and scoop it up into your body to keep it safe.

Shots at chest height

These are easy saves to make, if performed well. There are two techniques. The first is to cup your hands underneath the ball and bend your body to clutch the ball into your chest. For the second method, catch the ball with your fingers spread out and away from your body.

In both cases, keep your hands and fingers flexible so that they cushion the impact of the ball.

Taking high balls

Catch the ball at the highest possible point. The lower it drops, the more vulnerable you will be to a challenge. Maximum height will be gained with a one-footed take-off. The fingers should be spread wide and not too tense. Once the ball is in your hands, bring it down and into the chest as soon as possible.

Brilliant saves can win games but mistakes are often punished.

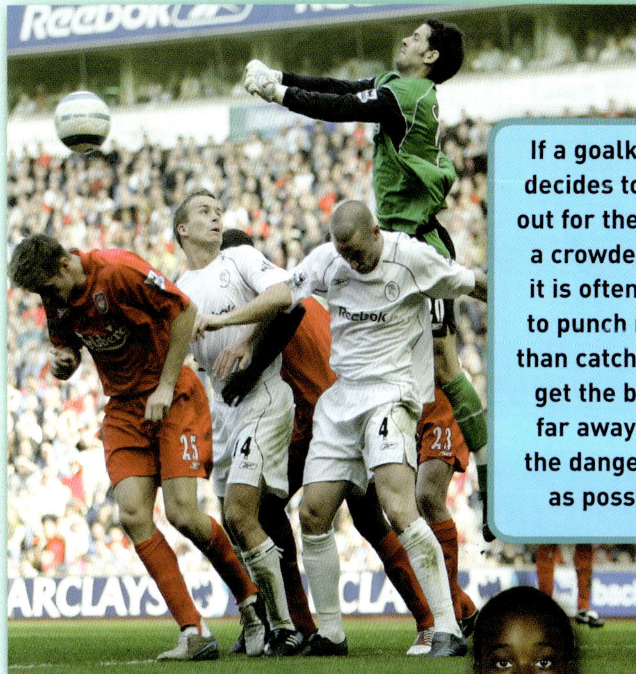

Scott Carson, the Liverpool goalkeeper, punches clear from Kevin Nolan and Kevin Davies of Bolton.

If a goalkeeper decides to come out for the ball in a crowded box, it is often safer to punch rather than catch. Try to get the ball as far away from the danger area as possible.

Diving

For shots wide of the keeper, where you are unable to get your body behind the ball, you may have to launch yourself to make a save. Push off with the leg nearest the ball and aim to get both hands on it if possible.

Catch, punch or deflect?

Catching the ball is best, but sometimes it may not be possible. If you are under pressure, a very firm punch, one- or two-handed, and through the middle of the ball, can send it out of danger. Be careful, though, of simply punching it back to the opposition. A deflection can stop a goal by guiding the ball round the post or over the bar. To deflect the ball, make contact with the open palm and outstretched fingers. Guide the ball over the bar or round the post. Take care not to get too full and firm a contact, as the ball might rebound back into danger.

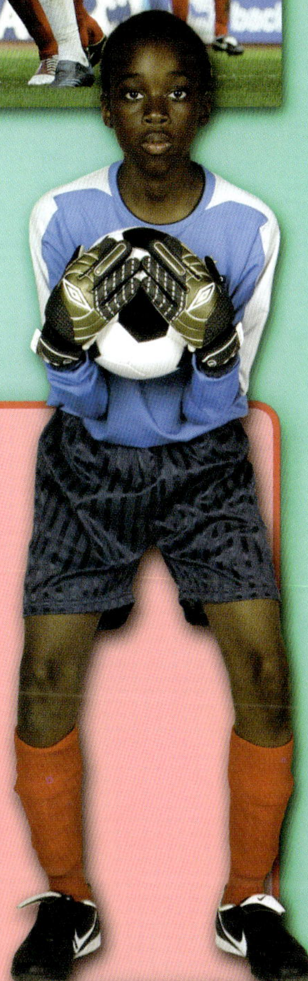

Quick reactions

Fast reactions and excellent handling skills are both things a good goalkeeper needs.

Waist height

Saves at between head and waist height can be made with hands pointing up or cupped underneath the ball.

Positional play

Goalkeepers should be constantly changing their position depending on where the ball is. When possible, the keeper should place him- or herself in a direct line between the ball and the centre of the goal.

Being in the right place at the right time is perhaps the goalkeeper's most important skill.

As well as moving to the left or right, the goalkeeper also has to be ready to go forwards. If an attacker is 'through on goal', as keeper you must aim to make yourself as big an obstacle as possible. At the same time, you will be limiting the attacker's view of the goal. Narrowing the angle is one of a keeper's range of vital weapons, but it isn't risk-free. If you advance too far or not far enough, too soon or too late, you will give the advantage to the attacker. The attacker might then pass, dribble past or go for a chip.

Good positioning can make difficult saves look quite easy. Being in the right place at the right time is perhaps the goalkeeper's most important skill, and probably the most difficult to learn. Good judgement only comes with experience and lots of work in training.

Back pass rule

A goalkeeper receiving a deliberate back pass is not allowed to pick up the ball.

An opponent closes the keeper down, hoping to pressure him into a miskick.

Jussi Jaaskelainen of Bolton Wanderers during a match against Blackburn Rovers.

Underarm throw

An underarm throw starts from a crouched position, with your front foot pointing towards your target. Bowl the ball out smoothly with your hand pointing in the ball's direction.

Distribution

The decision-making doesn't stop once a keeper has possession of the ball. He or she has to choose how to release the ball and distribute it to their team. Good decision-making and fast, accurate distribution can turn defence into attack. Keepers have a choice of short underarm throws or more powerful overarm and 'javelin' throws. They can also kick the ball from their hand to gain maximum distance. Keepers also have to be good at kicking a rolling ball because of the backpass rule, which stops them from picking up a ball deliberately passed back to them.

TIPS

- Be ready. Expect a shot or cross at all times.
- Stay well balanced with legs slightly bent.
- Watch the ball and get behind the line of flight where possible.
- If you cannot catch the ball, punch it as far as possible to give the attacking team less opportunity to follow up.
- Constantly communicate with your defenders. Remember that you have the best view of the play.
- Make sure the defender knows if you are going to come out and claim the ball.
- When diving keep your arms relaxed to absorb the impact.

Players defend a free kick in a Bundesliga match between Hertha BSC Berlin and Hamburger SV.

As a keeper, always make sure you have a good view of the ball. From free kicks it is often best to get a good view of your opponent kicking the ball rather than have your vision completely hidden by the defending wall.

SET PIECES

Robin van Persie beats the Ivory Coast wall to score for Holland at Germany 2006. Out of all set pieces, free kicks produce the greatest number of goals.

Throw-ins, corners, free kicks and penalties have two major advantages. First, the player taking the kick or throw is dealing with a stationary ball and is under less pressure. Second, set pieces can be practised endlessly on the training ground. Your teammates know exactly what is going to happen – where they have to move, whether they will receive the ball or be a decoy runner – and this gives you a great advantage over your opponents.

Set pieces tend to come from good attacking play. A goalkeeper or defender might, for example, deflect a shot that runs out for a corner or concede a penalty by fouling an attacker through on goal. Apart from attacking, set pieces are also generated when one team puts pressure on the team with the ball by chasing the ball down or harassing the player in possession of the ball into making a mistake or forcing them to kick the ball out of play.

Nearly half of all goals come directly or indirectly from set pieces. No team can afford to ignore such a rich source of goals.

Marking

At set pieces defenders should try to position themselves so that they can see both the player they are marking and the ball.

Brazil defend a corner during the women's football Olympic gold medal match.

Defending set pieces

As so many scoring chances and goals are created at set pieces, it is vital that the defending team do everything they can to prevent such chances occurring. Just as players practise taking set pieces, they also practise defending them. Players take their instructions from their goalkeeper and usually mark a particular opponent. The penalty area can get crowded, and defenders need to stay fully focused and ready to react to a quick move by the player they are marking.

Inswinging corners such as this will swerve the ball towards the goalmouth. The slightest contact – from an attacker or defender – might lead to a goal.

German Bundesliga match between FC Koeln and LR Ahlen.

Corners

Corners can be a rich source of scoring chances. They can be divided up in different ways. Corners can be taken short or long, and can be delivered to the far post, near post or middle of the goal. They can be bent inwards (inswing) or hit so that they bend outwards (outswing). Much depends on the corner taker to deliver an accurate ball at the right height and into the right area for his team. His teammates then have to time their runs and jumps and get free of their marker to make contact with the ball.

Inswing or outswing?

Outswinging corner kicks swerve away from the goalkeeper and defenders and can be met full-on by an attacker to send the ball goalwards with lots of power. Inswinging corners may be heading towards the goalkeeper, but attackers look to get some sort of touch with foot or head on them to send them into the goal. Both types of corners should be practised and used in games to keep the opposition guessing.

Be alert – a quick set piece can catch defenders off guard.

David Beckham sets up a free kick during a 2006 World Cup match between England and Ecuador.

Alessandro del Piero tries to bend the ball up and over a practice wall during a training session with the Italian national team.

The top players spend a lot of time practising free kicks. In a proper game, of course, there would be defenders out to stop you from scoring, so a dummy wall is often used on the training pitch.

Free kicks

When it comes to deciding whether to shoot (assuming that it's a direct free kick), the distance from goal and the angle will be the deciding factors. If the kick is too wide or too far out, then you should aim to get the ball into the danger area. Generally, that means playing the ball behind the last defender. Defenders like to play the ball in front of them; they hate turning and having to defend while facing their own goal, particularly if under pressure.

Darren Bent of Charlton fires in a free kick during a Premiership game against Newcastle United.

It is always a good idea to have two or three players lined up to take a free kick. Your team will know what is going to happen, but dummies and decoys will create confusion and uncertainty in the defence.

Choosing to shoot

For more central free kicks that are within striking range, the defending side have even more to worry about. They will usually put up a wall to give the goalkeeper extra protection. Of course, the attacking side are in a powerful position, and a chip or pass could take all the defenders in the wall out of the game. Having said that, most teams who get a direct free kick just outside the box will usually choose to shoot. This is because the 'move' involves just one touch from one player. As a rule, the more elaborate the free kick – that is, the more players and touches it involves – the more chance there is that it will go wrong.

Of all set plays, free kicks produce the greatest number of goals.

Play to your strengths

Not all sides have a David Beckham or Ronaldinho in them. Play to your own team's strengths. If you have players who are good at bending the ball, by all means use them. If you have someone with an explosive low drive, then you could set them up by playing the ball square. The same applies if you have players who are particularly strong in the air or who are good at timing their runs into the space behind the defence. The last two examples involve at least two players and two touches, and therefore will be very useful for indirect free kicks.

Throw-ins

In defensive positions the throw-in is usually used to restart the game and hold possession. In the attacking third, it can be a dangerous weapon. Many teams have a long-throw expert capable of reaching the near post, making this set piece as valuable as a corner. Even if you can't achieve such distances, you can still increase the attacking threat in a number of ways.

Long throw

Many teams have a long throw specialist who can reach the goalmouth, making it as good as a corner. Remember you must keep both feet on the ground, otherwise it's a foul throw.

- When you take a throw-in you should have more than one choice. If players are on the move then space can be created for the receiver.
- As soon as you have taken a throw-in, step back on to the pitch and be alert. Sometimes, the person who receives the throw may look to pass the ball straight back to you.
- Make life as easy as possible for the receiver. Your teammate won't appreciate a ball bouncing awkwardly, or delivered where their marker can easily challenge.
- Make the most of space. A ball thrown into space beyond a defender could set up a teammate to cross or shoot. There is no offside from a throw-in so attackers can make their run early.
- Quick throw-ins are more likely to catch defences off guard, and the nearest player should therefore take the throw-in. The exception to this is the long throw, when you might wait for the specialist in your team.

1.

The throw-in

Bend your knees and arch your back while keeping good balance. Take the ball right back between your shoulder blades for maximum leverage. Release the ball as it passes in front of your head. Spread your hands around the back and sides of the ball so that your thumbs almost touch. This gives you good grip of the football.

2.

Many games are won and lost on penalty kicks, particularly in tournaments where shoot-outs are used if the score is level after extra-time. When taking a penalty, make your mind up whether you are going to place the ball or go for power, then stick to your decision.

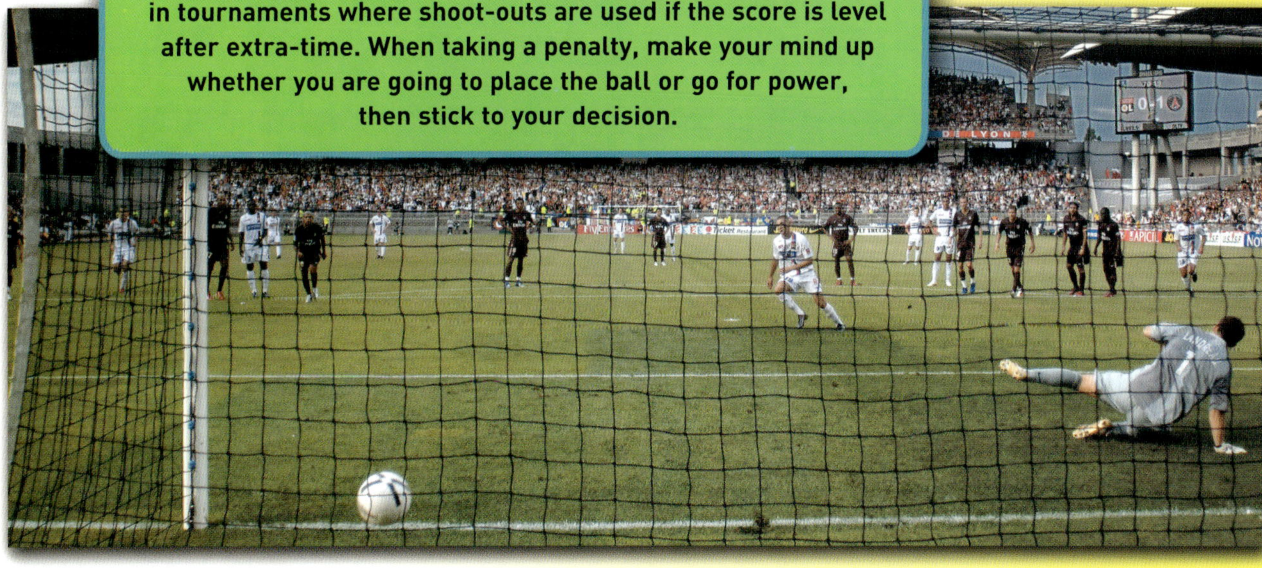

French forward Karim Benzema scores a penalty during a Champions Trophy match.

Penalties

Penalties are increasingly important in football. A side awarded a penalty often celebrate as if a goal has already been scored. Although a penalty is an excellent chance of scoring, and the penalty taker has a better chance of scoring than the keeper has of saving, there is still work to be done.

With expectation comes pressure, and some players find what should be a simple shot from less than 12 metres away, with only the keeper to beat, is too much for them. Players who handle the pressure best are often good penalty takers.

A penalty taker has a number of choices to make about where to hit the ball, with what sort of shot and with how much force. Some players prefer power, and choose to blast the ball with an instep drive aimed at the middle of the goal. Others prefer to place the ball using a controlled instep drive or firm sidefoot shot low into the corners of the net.

TIPS

Penalty taking:

- Decide in advance how and where you are going to hit your penalty.
- Relax, and just think about getting your shot on target.
- If you are uncertain where to aim, go for the corners of the goal.
- Don't let the keeper's movement along the line or any comments or tricks from your opponents distract you.
- If you miss a penalty, don't worry. Forget about it and continue playing. Even the most talented players miss penalties.

Penalty shoot-outs

Penalty shoot-outs are used to settle drawn matches in some competitions. Five players per side are picked to take a penalty each. If the scores are level after all ten penalties are taken, the competition goes into 'sudden death' with pairs of players, one from each side, taking penalties until one team wins. Many games in the World Cup Finals have been decided on penalties. England have suffered badly, having gone out of World Cups in 1990, 1998 and 2006 because they lost penalty shoot-outs.

GLOSSARY

Block tackle Where a player challenges for the ball on the ground by using the side of the foot.

Chip A stabbing move down behind the ball to make it rise steeply.

Cushioning Allowing the part of the body receiving the ball to relax and move backwards in order to take the pace off the ball.

Dragback A dribbling trick where you place your foot on top of the ball and draw it back to beat an opponent. A double dragback involves doing the same move twice in quick succession, usually with the opposite foot the second time.

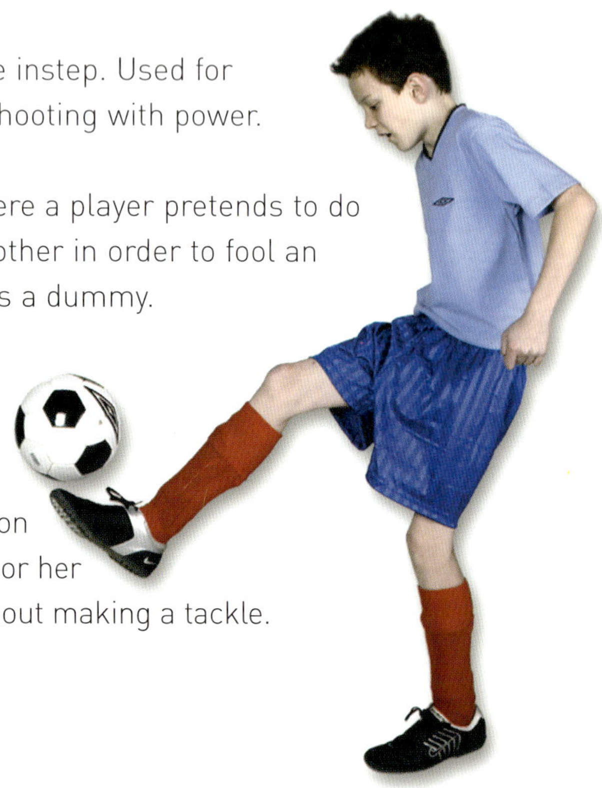

Drive Striking the ball with the instep. Used for long-range passing or shooting with power.

Feint Any body movement where a player pretends to do one thing, then does another in order to fool an opponent. Also known as a dummy.

Inswinger A cross or corner that curls towards the goal.

Jockeying Closing down the player on the ball and delaying his or her progress legally, but without making a tackle.

Nutmeg Beating your opponent by playing the ball through his or her legs.

Outswinger A cross or corner that curls away from the goal.

Push pass Striking the ball with the side of the foot. Despite its name, this technique is equally important when it comes to shooting.

Set piece A move practised by a team to use at a dead-ball situation such as a free kick, corner or throw-in.

Shielding Keeping your body between an opponent and the ball.

Step-over A dribbling trick where you feint to play the ball in one direction, then take your foot over the ball and move off in another direction.

Swerving Bending the ball by striking it off-centre.

Volley Striking the ball with the foot when it is in the air.

Wall pass A passing move to beat an opponent, sometimes known as a 'one-two'. One player passes to a teammate and runs into a space beyond the opponent to receive the return pass.

Warm-down Jogging and stretching at the end of a game to relax the muscles and prevent them from stiffening up.

Warm-up A pre-match exercise routine to prepare the body for vigorous physical activity.

INDEX

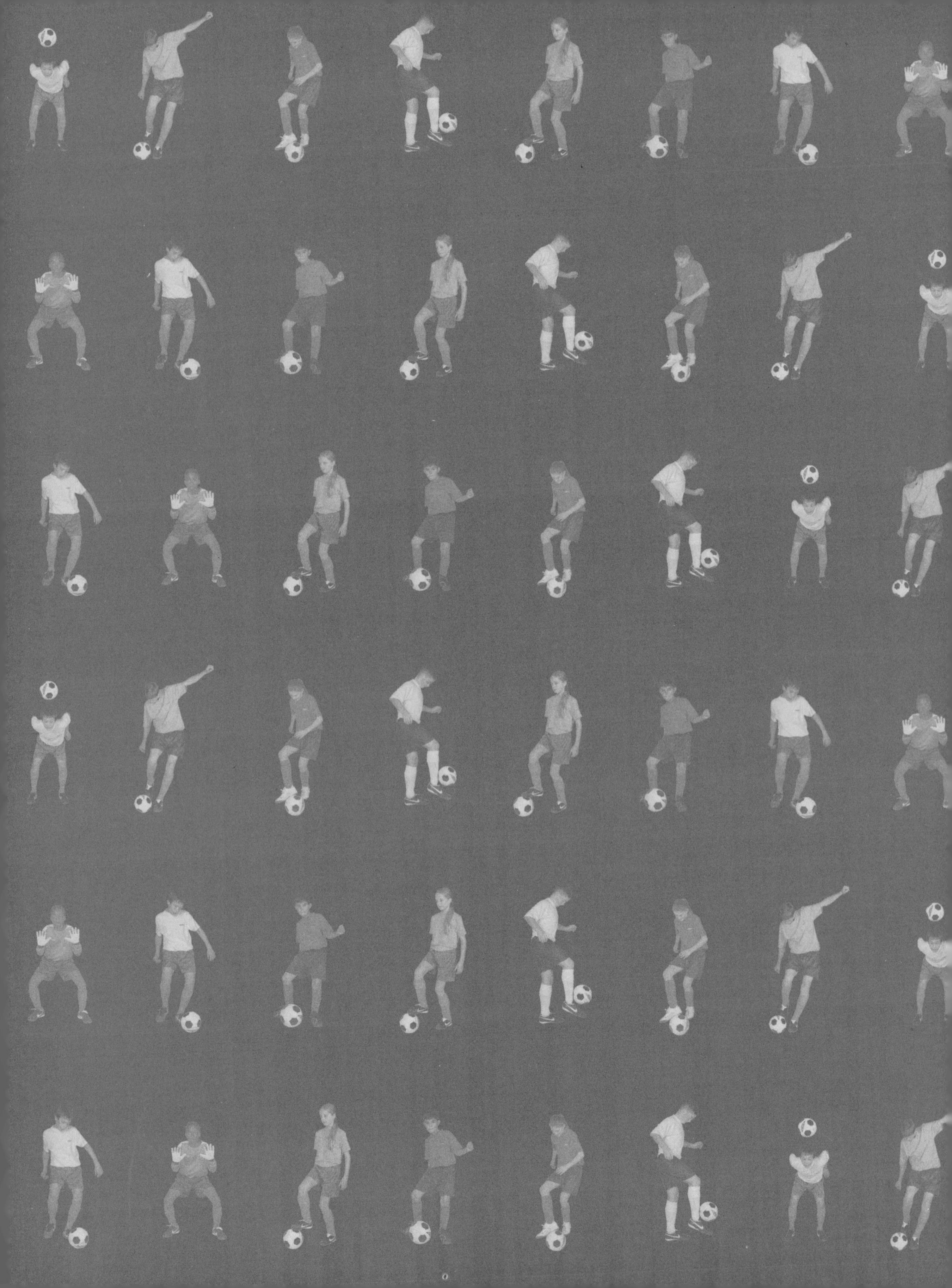